McDougal Littell

TEST GENERATOR
User's Guide

version 3.0

For use with Test Generator

Help with...

- Creating, saving, and printing tests
- Editing test items
- Adding your own test items
- Formatting tests
- Searching for test items correlated to standards
- Online Test Delivery

This User's Guide for McDougal Littell Test Generator is also provided for you in PDF form under the Help menu in the tool bar of your Test Generator software. The guide can be read or printed with Adobe Acrobat Reader. Use the paging arrows or scroll bars to go to pages of the guide. Choose Print in the File menu of Adobe Acrobat Reader to print out any or all of the guide.

For help with McDougal Littell Test Generator call 1-800-727-3009 between 9:00 am and 8:00 pm EST Monday through Thursday, and between 9:00 am and 5:00 pm EST on Friday, or visit www.mcdougallittell.com and click on State Resources for updated state standard correlations, troubleshooting information, and patches. For more information about McDougal Littell products, call 1-800-462-6595, or visit www.mcdougallittell.com.

XMLmind Spell-Checker Copyright © 2002 Pixware SARL.

Adobe, Acrobat, and the Acrobat logo are trademarks of Adobe Systems, Inc.

Copyright © by McDougal Littell, a division of Houghton Mifflin Company. All rights reserved.

Permission is hereby granted to classroom teachers to print and photocopy the output files from this software for school use only. Such copies may not be sold, and further distribution is expressly prohibited. Except as authorized above, prior written permission must be obtained from McDougal Littell, a division of Houghton Mifflin Company, to reproduce or transmit this work or portions thereof in any other form or by any other electronic or mechanical means, including information storage or retrieval systems, unless expressly permitted by federal copyright law. Address inquiries to Supervisor, Rights and Permissions, McDougal Littell, a division of Houghton Mifflin Company, P.O. Box 1667, Evanston, Illinois 60204.

ISBN-13: 978-0-618-37372-7   ISBN-10: 0-618-37372-1

16 - CKI - 09 08 07

User's Guide Contents

INTRODUCTION 1
  Note to Previous Test Generator Users 1

INSTALLING TEST GENERATOR 2
  Windows System 2
  Macintosh System 3

QUICK START GUIDE 4
  Starting Test Generator 4
  Selecting a Test 5
  Printing a Test 6

TEST GENERATOR OVERVIEW 7
  Useful Terms 7

TEST GENERATOR TOOL BAR AND MENUS 7
  Tool Bar 8
  File menu 8
  Edit menu 9
  Test menu 10
  Tools menu 10
  Help menu 10

OPENING QUESTION BANKS AND TESTS 11

BUILDING YOUR OWN TEST 12
  Viewing a Question Bank 12
  Types of Questions 13
  Question Summary 13
  Adding and Removing Questions 14
  Adding Multiple Questions 14
  Removing Multiple Questions 15

ENTERING YOUR OWN QUESTIONS 15
  Adding Questions to the Question Bank 15
  Copy Questions/Editing Questions 17
  Editing Instructions 18
  Deleting Questions/Saving Changes/Sort in Book Order 19
  Find Questions Using the Search Question Bank 19
  Viewing Standards 20
  Formatting Your Test 21
  Preview Test 23
  Insert Page Break Into Test 23
  Exporting a Test 24

CHANGING A QUESTION BANK 25
  Creating a New Test Folder/Importing Tests 25
  Editing Question Banks 26

SAVING TESTS 26
  Opening Saved Tests 26

PRINTING TESTS 26
  Preview/Print 27

HELP AND TECHNICAL ASSISTANCE 27

Introduction

McDougal Littell Test Generator allows you to create and print tests from prepared Question Banks. Use Test Generator to quickly create custom tests that include specific types of questions and those correlated to particular state or national standards. Questions you have written can be entered and imported into Test Generator.

When you print a test for students, Test Generator delivers a professionally-formatted test, complete with headings, instructions, images, and answer keys. Tests are printed directly from Test Generator when you select Print Test from the File Menu. While most of the work is done for you, Test Generator gives you the option of customizing your printouts, including creating multiple versions of tests.

NOTE TO PREVIOUS TEST GENERATOR USERS:

If you have an older version (version 1.0, 1.5, or 2.0) of the McDougal Littell Test Generator, you may continue with installation of the new 3.0 version. Version 3.0 will automatically convert any earlier version's books or tests for use with version 3.0. The conversion will take place once per book or test, and will occur upon opening that book or test for the first time with the new software. **To ensure smooth conversion, take care to install version 3.0 in the same place you had the previous version installed.** When printing an older version of a test with your new software for the first time, you may want to preview and adjust manual page breaks or other formatting, as newer versions may handle printing differently.

To install and begin using Test Generator, follow the instructions on the following pages.

Installing Test Generator

WINDOWS® SYSTEM

Operating System: Windows 98, NT, 2000, ME, or XP

Free Disk Storage Space: Approximately 100 MB, depending on the actual number of Test Generator Question Banks and standards installed

Memory: 32MB, 64MB recommended

Processor: Pentium

INSTALLATION

1. Insert the Test Generator CD into your CD-ROM drive. Double click the **My Computer** icon on your desktop to display the items on your computer.
2. Double click the **McDougal Littell** icon to open it. (Read the readme.txt file if you like.) Double click the **Setup.exe**.
3. Click **Next** on the program's title and the setup note screens.
4. After reading the License Agreement, click Yes to continue. Click No to cancel installation. You can also choose to print or save the License Agreement for future reference.
5. Select the directory to which Test Generator will be installed. The install program suggests C:\Program Files\TestGen, but you can enter a different directory name or select a directory using the **Browse** button. If you have an older version of the McDougal Littell Test Generator, make sure that you install to the same location in order to convert any books or tests.
6. Enter the two-letter abbreviation for your state to include state or national standards that may be correlated to the Question Bank you are installing. Click **OK**.
7. A folder titled **McDougal Littell Test Generator** will be installed according to your selections.
8. Click **Close** on the display that reports the completion of the installation.

MACINTOSH® SYSTEM

Operating System: Mac OS 8.6 through 10.3

Free Disk Storage Space: Approximately 80 MB, depending on the actual number of Test Generator Question Banks and standards installed

Memory: 32MB, 64MB recommended

Processor: PowerPC

INSTALLATION

1. Insert the Test Generator CD into a CD-ROM drive. Double click the **McDougal Littell** CD icon to open it. (Read the readme.txt file if you like.)

2. Double click the **Setup** icon.

3. Click **Continue** on the program's title screen. After reading the License Agreement, click **Accept** to continue. Click **Decline** to cancel installation. You can also choose to print or save the License Agreement for future reference.

4. Click **Continue** on the installation note. You can also choose to print or save the note for future reference.

5. Select the location where Test Generator will be installed. You can choose Easy Install to have all components of Test Generator saved on your computer. If you choose Custom Install, you can choose to install Macintosh Runtime for Java if you do not have it. Java is required to run the Test Generator program. Click **Install** to continue. If you have an older version of the McDougal Littell Test Generator, make sure that you install to the same location in order to convert any books or tests.

6. Enter the two-letter abbreviation for your state to include state or national standards that may be correlated to the Question Bank you are installing. Click **OK**.

7. A folder titled **McDougal Littell Test Generator** will be installed according to your selections.

8. Macintosh Runtime for Java will then be installed if you have chosen to include it. If the install program detects a version of Java already on your computer, you will be asked if you want to continue with its installation. Make your selection to continue.

9. Click **OK** on the display screen that reports the completion of the installation.

Quick Start Guide

The easiest way to use Test Generator is to select and print a prepared test for a McDougal Littell book from the Question Bank. This Quick Start guide gives you a quick introduction on how to start the Test Generator and quickly create and print a test. More detailed instructions are available in later sections of this User's Guide (beginning on page 7).

STARTING TEST GENERATOR ON WINDOWS

1. Click the **Start** button in the lower left corner of your computer's screen.
2. Highlight **Programs** menu from the popup list, and all the programs installed on your computer will be displayed.
3. Highlight **McDougal Littell Test Generator** and select the application called **Teacher.**
4. Choose a McDougal Littell book from the list and click **Open** to load its Question Bank. Data for a Question Bank can take from several seconds to a few minutes to load, depending on your system and the bank's information.

STARTING TEST GENERATOR ON MACINTOSH

1. For Macintosh systems, double click your hard drive icon.
2. Open the **McDougal Littell Test Generator** folder.
3. Double click the **Teacher** icon to begin.
4. Choose a McDougal Littell book from the list and click **Open** to load its Question Bank. Data for a book can take from several seconds to a few minutes to load, depending on your system and the book's information.

SELECTING A TEST

- Begin Test Generator and select the Question Bank you want to open.

- On the left side of the Test Generator main screen, click the right pointing arrow (▶), or double click the folder icon of the Question Bank to open it. Open a section of the Question Bank by clicking its arrow. Continue to open sections until you see the test folder and/or test questions you want.

- To select all the questions in the test, drag the test folder to the blank area tab titled **Your Test** on the right side of the screen. The program will ask: Add all questions from this section to the test? Click Yes to go on.

- Once test questions have been entered into the **Your Test** tab, the total number of questions will display in parentheses above the test.

- You can delete a question by clicking on the question and then choosing Remove in the **Question Options** box at the bottom. The up and down pointing arrows allow you to move questions up and down within the test.

- Choose Format Test from Test Options, the Tool Bar icon, or the File Menu to make any font, margin, spacing, or header and footer changes.

- When you are finished, click **Save Test** from the File Menu, the Tool Bar, or Test Options. In the **Save Test Generator Test As** screen, enter a name for the file and click **Save.**

- After saving a test, you may print it at any time. If you wish to leave Test Generator, select **Exit** from the File menu. Verify that you are sure you want to exit by clicking **Yes.**

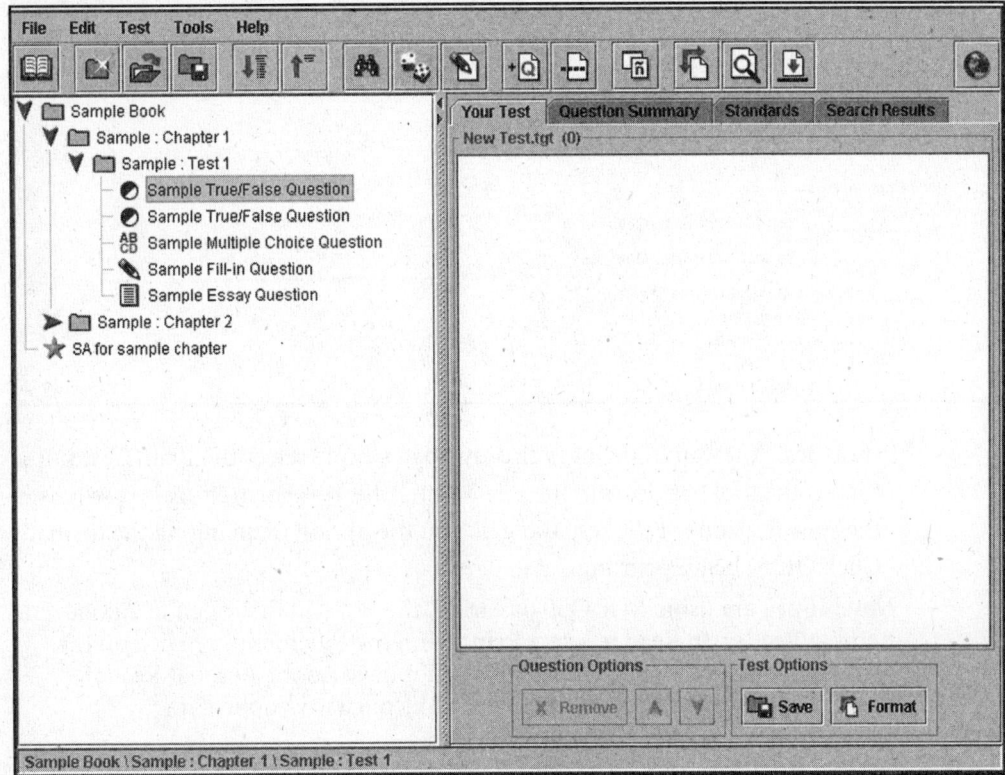

TEST GENERATOR USER'S GUIDE   5

PRINTING A TEST

- If your test is not open click the Open Test button in the File Menu or on the tool bar. You will see the contents of the Tests folder in the McDougal Littell Test Generator folder on your hard drive. If you have saved your test in a different location, make selections in the dialog box to locate it. Click the Open button to open the test.

- After Test Generator reads the test, it will be displayed in the **Your Test** tab.

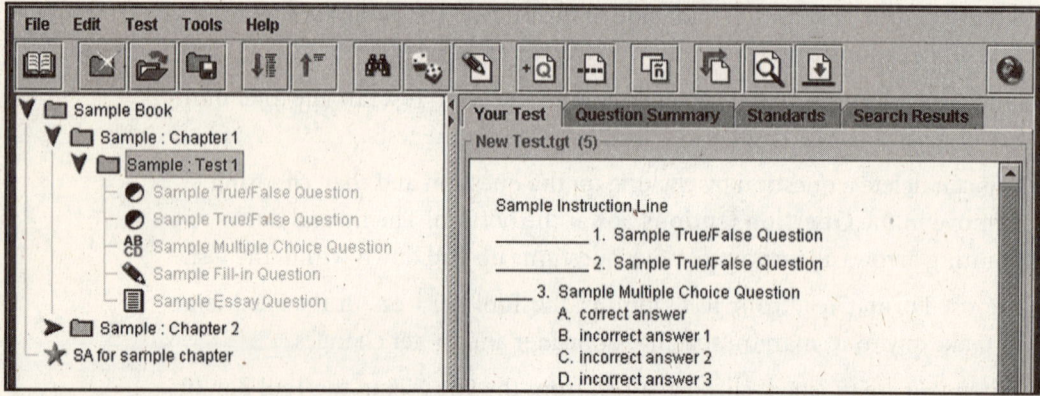

- Click the **Preview Test** button on the tool bar or from the File Menu to view the test as it is formatted.

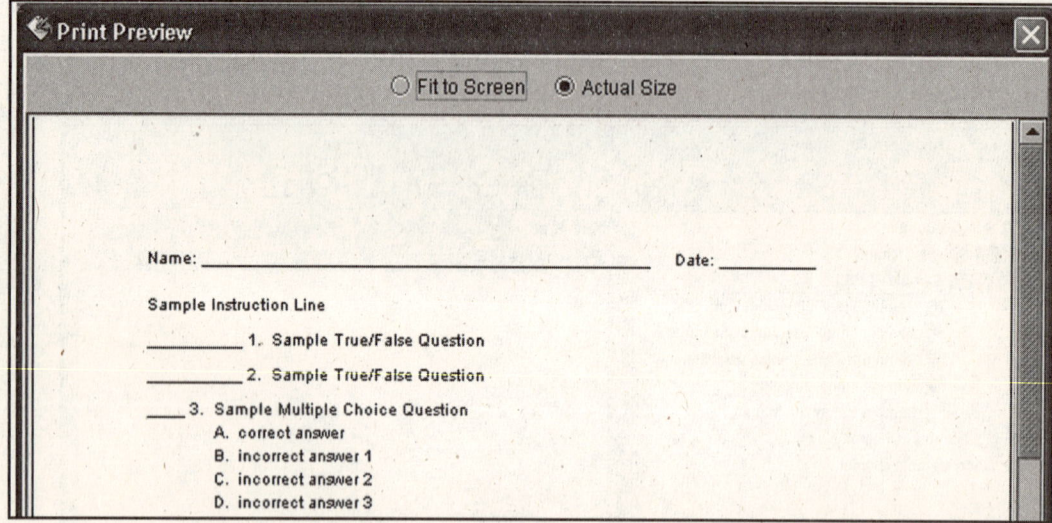

- If the test you want to print is already open simply select the **Print Test** button on the tool bar or from the File Menu. The Test Formatting box will list the specifications of the test and give you the option of changing the format. Click **OK** to begin printing.

Note: If you are using Mac OS9 or earlier, the test will first open in Adobe Acrobat Reader. In Reader, select **Print** from the **File** menu, or click on the printer icon to print your test. If you do not have Adobe Acrobat Reader installed, you may download it for free at http://www.adobe.com.

- When you are ready to quit Test Generator, select **Exit** from the File menu. If you have made changes to the test, you will be asked if you want to save it. Click **Yes** to save your changes.

Test Generator Overview

McDougal Littell Test Generator allows you to create a test from Question Banks, enter your own questions, and print custom tests. To see more information about these options, go to the corresponding pages in this guide.

The Tools menu gives you the option of seeing the main screen in either a vertical or a horizontal view. This menu also helps you to search the Question Bank for questions to add to your test or allows you to build a test randomly with the **Add Random Questions** tool.

USEFUL TERMS

Question Bank refers to a McDougal Littell textbook and its collection of questions that are organized into tests according to the book's chapters or units. From the Question Bank, you can build a test and enter your own questions.

Edit Menu allows you to enter your own questions, edit questions, and create new test folders in which to place your questions.

Exhibits are graphics, images, or long text passages that accompany questions. They are files saved in either the GIF of JPEG format.

The **Search Question Bank** tool helps you search the Question Bank for questions that are of a certain format, contain specific words or phrases, or are correlated to certain standards.

Keywords are words you enter to index questions by categories.

Standards are state or local curriculum guides that may be correlated to questions in the Question Bank you are using.

Tool Bar is the set of buttons just below the Test Generator menus that allow you to perform many key functions: Open Question Bank, New Test, Open Test, Save Test, Expand Question Bank, Collapse Question Bank, Search Question Bank, Add Random Questions, Edit Question, Add Question to Test, Insert Page Break Into Test, Copy Special Characters, Format Test, Preview Test, Print Test and McDougal Littell on The Web.

Question Options allows you to remove a question from your test or change a question's position in the test.

Test Options allows you to save a test or change its format.

Test Generator Tool Bar and Menus

Detailed information on using the Test Generator tool bar and menus is provided throughout this guide. In this section, a summary of each button and menu item is provided. Because Test Generator is a flexible program, there is often more than one way to accomplish the same function. You can choose the method that best suits you.

TOOL BAR

The tool bar is located at the top of the screen just under the menu bar. There are 16 icons that provide shortcuts to frequently-used options. Moving your mouse over each item without clicking displays the button label.

Open Question Bank loads a bank of questions that you have installed.

New Test clears the information in the Your Test tab and allows you to start building another test.

Open Test loads a test you have previously saved.

Save Test saves a file with the information in the Your Test tab.

Expand Question Bank opens all folders and shows all questions in the Question Bank.

Collapse Question Bank closes all folders in the Question Bank.

Search Question Bank searches either the Entire Bank or the Current Section of the Question Bank for questions to add to your test.

Add Random Questions randomly selects questions according to your specifications and adds them to your test.

Edit Question allows you to enter and change any part of a question you add or copy.

Add Question to Test places the current highlighted question into the Your Test tab.

Insert Page Break into Test is used to add a manual page break to a test when it is printed.

Copy Special Characters This function allows you to place upper- or lower-case special characters (such as é, ñ, ü, etc.) into your text when you are in Edit Question mode.

Format Test provides many options for you to control how the test will look when it is printed. Use this command to change margins, spacing between questions, font size, and many other specifications.

Preview Test displays your formatted test as it will look when printed.

Print Test allows you to print your finished test.

McDougal Littell On The Web launches McDougal Littell's website. Your computer must have an active internet connection.

FILE MENU

The File menu is the first menu at the top of McDougal Littell Test Generator window. Use the commands in the File menu to work with Question Banks, test files, printing, saving, and exiting Test Generator.

Open Question Bank loads a bank of questions that you have installed.

Save Question Bank saves changes you have made to the Question Bank.

New Test clears the information in the Your Test tab and allows you to start building another test.

Open Test loads a test you have previously saved.

Save Test saves a file with the information in the Your Test tab.

Save Test As saves a file and gives you the option of changing the location and name of the test file.

Import lets you load questions from a word processing file that you have marked up.

Export Test to Text writes the current test in the Your Test tab into a file that can be opened with your word processor.

Export Test to PDF saves the current test as a .pdf file that can be read with Adobe Acrobat Reader. Allows you to move tests from computer to computer without having the Test Generator application installed.

Export to EasyPlanner allows you to incorporate a saved test into a lesson plan created with the McDougal Littell EasyPlanner CD-ROM.

Export Bank to Text places all of the questions in the Question Bank of a highlighted folder into a file that can be opened with your word processor. Caution: a Question Bank may contain over 3000 questions. To export a smaller number of items, first build a test with a subset of questions and export the test.

Open Exported Text and **Open Exported PDF** options allow you to launch any of the exported tests you have saved straight from Test Generator.

Format Test provides many options for you to control how the test will look when it is printed. Use this command to change margins, spacing between questions, font size, and many other specifications.

Preview Test shows you the test as it will appear as a printout.

Print Test prints your completed test.

Publish Your Test On-line is a premium McDougal Littell service. See the help menu of your Test Generator program for more information.

Exit quits the program.

EDIT MENU

The Edit menu lets you enter your own questions, edit questions, and create new test folders in which to place your questions. These commands allow you to make changes to the questions in the Question Bank.

Add Essay Question

Add Fill-in Question

Add Matching Question

Add Multiple Choice Question

Add True/False Question

Add Modified Matching Question

With these six commands, you are able to add each type of question to the Question Bank.

Copy Question copies a highlighted question and opens an edit box to allow you to make any changes.

Edit Question allows you to change any part of a question you add or copy.

Delete Question removes a question from the Question Bank. This is a permanent action, once you delete a question from the main Question Bank it cannot be retrieved.

Add Section adds a new folder to the Question Bank.

Rename Section renames a section of the Question Bank you have added.

Delete Section deletes a section of the Question Bank that you have added after all the questions have been deleted.

TEST MENU

The Test menu provides commands that help you build your test.

Add Question places the current highlighted question into the Your Test tab.

Insert Page Break allows you to manually choose where a new page of the test should begin when it is printed.

Sort In Book Order reorders questions in the Your Test tab by putting the questions in the same order they display in the Question Bank.

TOOLS MENU

The Tools menu both helps you find questions for your test and changes the way your test is displayed on the screen.

Search Question Bank searches either the entire bank or the current section of the bank for questions to add to your test.

Add Random Questions randomly selects questions according to your specifications and adds them to your test.

View Tall adds a vertical split to the screen. In this layout, the Question Bank is on the left side of the screen, and the test tabs are on the right.

View Wide adds a horizontal split to the screen. In this layout, the Question Bank is on the top of the screen, and the test tabs are on the bottom.

View Default returns all layout configurations to their original settings.

HELP MENU

The Help menu will guide you through the steps to creating your test.

User's Guide contains a copy of this guide in PDF format. You will need to install Adobe Acrobat Reader to be able to read this file.

Importing Instructions explains how to mark up files in a word processor which can then be imported into the Test Generator using the Import option under the File menu.

eTest Instructions provides information about eTest Plus Online, a premium service from McDougal Littell.

Tutorials will walk you through an Overview of Test Generator, as well as the steps to Opening a Bank and Creating a Test, Formatting and Printing the Test, Adding Your Own Test Item, Editing an Existing Test Item, Searching for Specific Test Items.

Quick Start gives you simple 1. 2. 3. . . . text instructions on Opening a Bank and Creating a Test, Formatting and Printing the Test, Adding Your Own Test Item, Editing an Existing Test Item, Editing Instructions, Searching for Specific Test Items, and Keyboard Navigation.

The **Icon Legend** identifies the icon for each question type. You can leave this legend open while you work. Simply use your mouse to move the legend to a convenient place on the screen.

McDougal Littell On The Web launches McDougal Littell's website. Your computer must have an active internet connection.

Opening Question Banks and Tests

With Test Generator you can easily create tests using McDougal Littell Question Banks and questions you have created. This section provides information about opening Question Banks and creating tests.

OPENING QUESTION BANKS

When you start Test Generator, choose the Question Bank you want to open, click the bank name to highlight it, and click **Open.** If you are using Test Generator for more than one Question Bank, open them by holding the Ctrl or Shift key as you click on each name. Each Question Bank you open can take from several seconds to a few minutes to load.

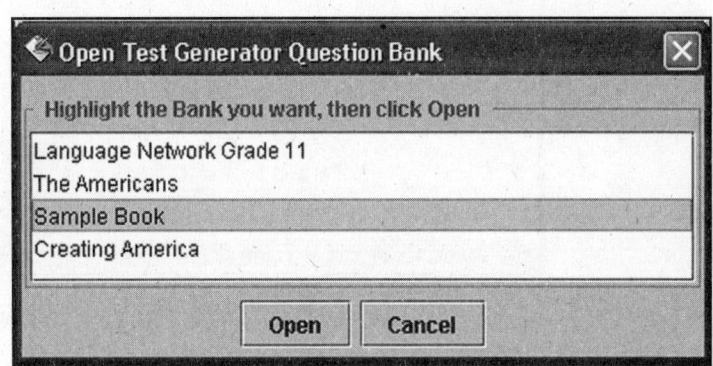

To open an additional Question Bank, you can always choose Open Question Bank from the File menu or click the **Open Question Bank** button in the tool bar.

OPENING TESTS

If you previously created a test and saved it, you can quickly open it using **Open Test** from the File menu or clicking the Open Test button in the tool bar. Next, select the name of the previously saved test from a list of all saved tests on your computer. Once you open the test, you can continue to make changes to it.

TEST GENERATOR USER'S GUIDE **11**

If you have created and printed a test, it is automatically saved in a TGT folder. These formatted tests can be saved to a diskette and taken to another computer installed with Test Generator and the same Question Bank.

Building Your Own Test

McDougal Littell Test Generator makes it easy for you to build custom tests for students. Many McDougal Littell textbook programs include Question Banks that cover the content with a variety of test formats. The test items in the McDougal Littell Test Generator may also be correlated to state or national standards. With Test Generator, you are able to build a test with just the questions you wish to include, change questions, or create your own questions.

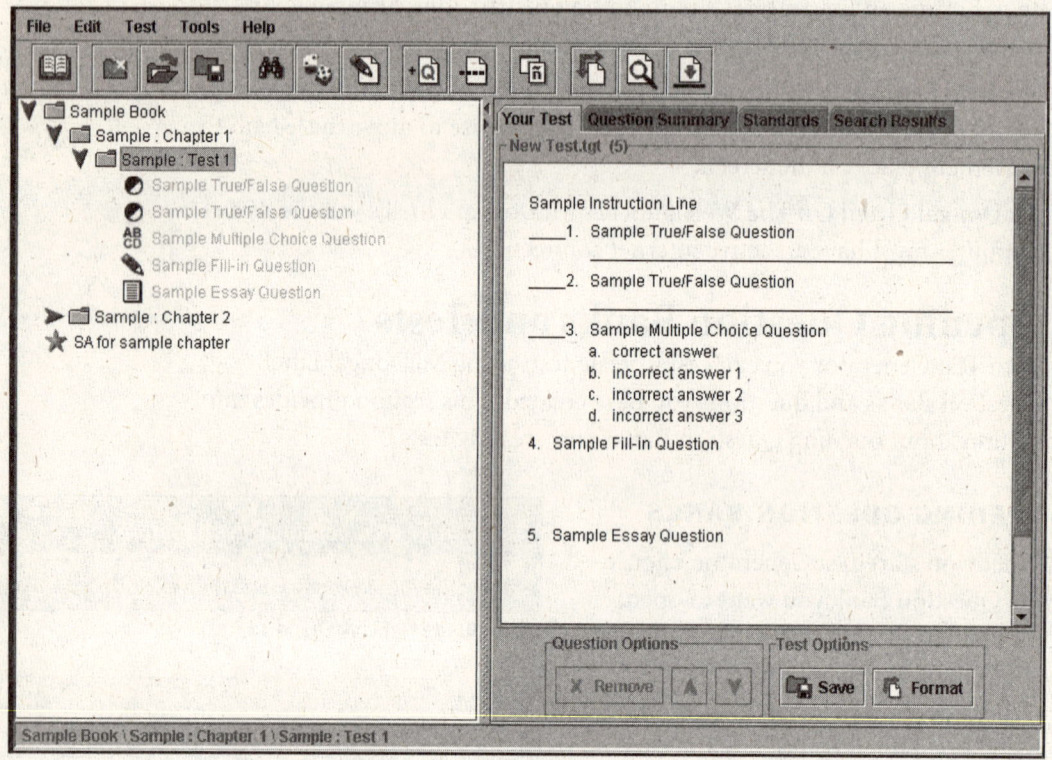

VIEWING A QUESTION BANK

McDougal Littell Test Generator is organized so that you can view both the Question Bank and your test simultaneously.

The Test Generator is divided into two panes: the left pane displays the Question Bank name and folders, and the right pane displays detailed information about your test.

By clicking on the arrows ▶ next to a folder, you can get a more detailed view of the contents in that folder. The Question Bank name is the top level of the hierarchy, and test items are the lowest level of the hierarchy. You can use the ▶ and ▼ arrows to quickly expand and collapse the hierarchy, so you can work with just the folders and test items you need. You can also use the **Expand Question Bank** and **Collapse Question Bank** buttons on the toolbar to quickly open or close all folders in the question bank.

The starred items beneath the Question Bank name are the sets of state or national standards that are correlated to test items for the open book.

TYPES OF QUESTIONS

When you see the individual questions in the Question Bank, the icon before each one gives you a quick visual reference of the question type. Questions you edit or add are designated with the apple icon.

Note: Not all Question Banks will have all types of questions.

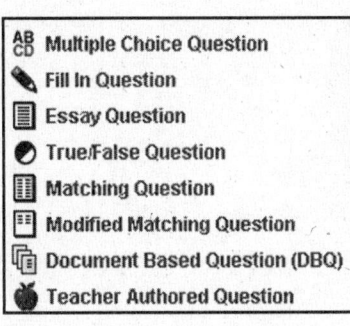

QUESTION SUMMARY

You should review questions in detail before placing them into your test. Click the Question Summary tab on the right side of the screen to bring it to the front. Highlight any question in the test folder to see information about the question. You may need to use the scroll bar on the right side of the **Question Summary** to see all the information. You may slide the center bar to the left or right depending on how much information you need to see. Hold your mouse over the bar until you see a double arrow, then hold down your mouse and drag in either direction. If you prefer to work with the screen in a horizontal position you may do so. Simply choose **View Wide** from the Tools menu. To return all screens to their original positions, choose **View Default** from the Tools menu.

Besides giving the full text of the question, the Question Summary displays all parts of each question: the instruction, points, exhibit (e.g. a graphic file), answer(s), keywords, difficulty level, and standards. Not all questions will use all of these parts.

The **instruction** gives students directions for the question, such as "Write the letter of the term that best matches the correct answer."

The **points** value shows the default value for questions in a test, such as "(4 points each)".

The **exhibit** is a graphic, table, text, or diagram students need to use to answer one or more questions. For instance, students might view a map and answer questions about it.

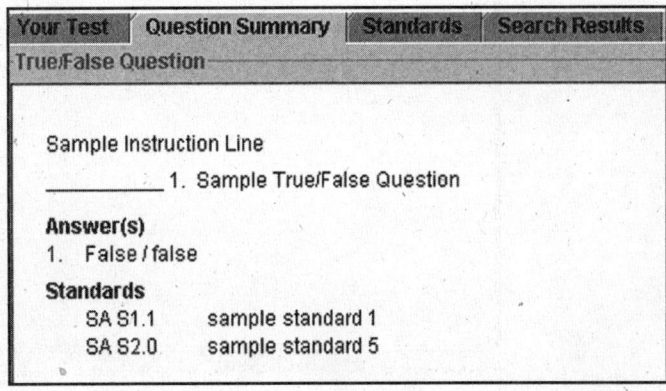

The **answer** lists the correct answer or possible answers.

Keywords are used to index questions.

Difficulty level shows the difficulty of the question, such as "Basic" or "Advanced".

TEST GENERATOR USER'S GUIDE   13

The state or national **standards** that may be correlated to the question are listed in this summary. These standards display under Keywords when you copy or edit a question.

ADDING AND REMOVING QUESTIONS

There are several ways to add questions to a test. Select a question you would like in your test. Then, click on the Test menu and choose **Add Question**, click on Add Question to Test in the tool bar, or use the keyboard shortcut. You can also use your mouse to drag the question to your test. You can add questions from any folder in a Question Bank or from different Question Banks. As you add questions, the total number of test questions will be displayed. Questions you add to your test are dimmed or shown in gray in the Question Bank. If you accidentally try to add the same question to a test twice, you will see a warning message alerting you that you have already added the question to the test.

To remove a question from your test, select it and click the **Remove** button in the Question Options box in the lower part of the screen. The question will no longer be dimmed in the Question Bank.

ADDING MULTIPLE QUESTIONS

You can add more than one question at a time to your test. To add an entire folder's questions, just click on the folder, then drag it into your test (or select **Add Question to Test** from the tool bar).

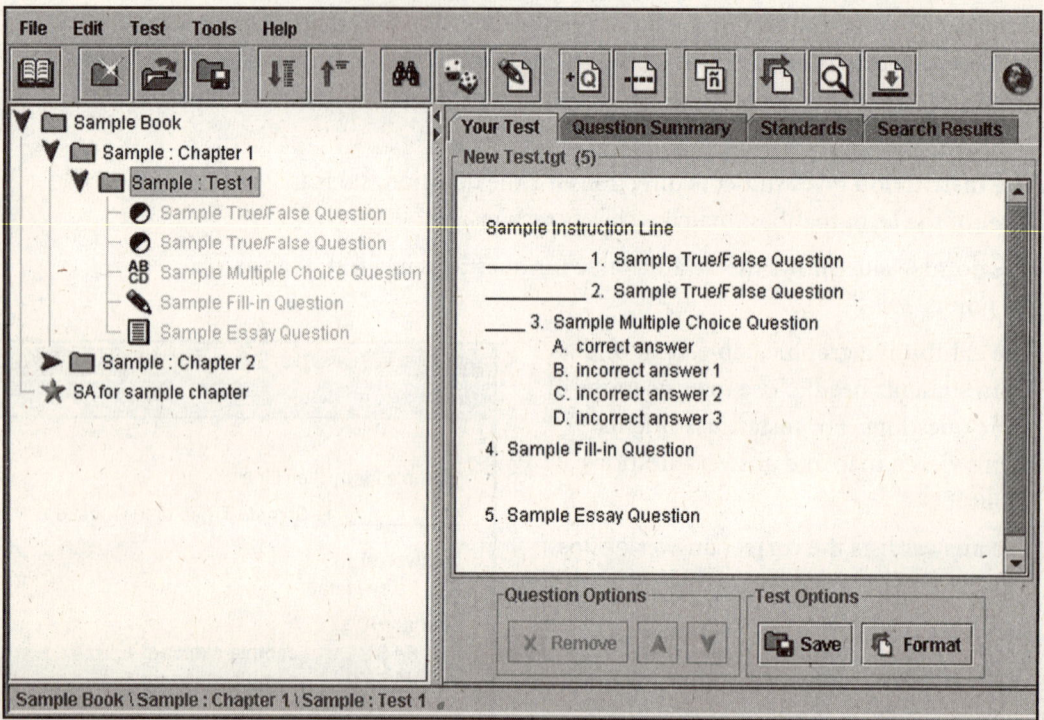

14 TEST GENERATOR USER'S GUIDE

You can also use the Shift key to select a continuous range of questions. Hold down the Shift key and click on the first question in the range of questions to add. Keep the Shift key held and click on the last question in the range. Then choose **Add Question to Test** from the tool bar.

If you want to add multiple questions that are not in a continuous range you can use the Control (Ctrl) key. Hold down the Control key and click on each question you want to add. Then choose Add Question to Test from the tool bar.

You can have Test Generator randomly select questions to add to your test. Click on **Add Random Questions** in the tool bar and Test Generator will search for questions from either the selected Question Bank or the Entire Question Bank. Click Done to add the questions to your test. Test Generator will prevent you from adding the same question twice.

The **Search Question Bank** tool will search either the current section of the Question Bank or the Entire Bank for questions that include the words or phrases you supply. You can also select the learning standards you want the questions to address. Simply click on Search Question Bank in the tool bar, add your specifications when prompted, and click on Done. The questions will display on the right side of the screen. To choose a question for your test, highlight it and then click Add to Test.

REMOVING MULTIPLE QUESTIONS

You can also remove more than one question from your test at a time. To remove a continuous range of questions, hold down the Shift Key and click on the first question of the range to remove in the Your Test tab. Keep the Shift key held and click on the last question in the range. Then click the Remove button in the Question Options box in the lower part of the screen.

If you want to remove questions that are not in a continuous range, you can use the Control (Ctrl) key. Hold down the Control key and click on each question you want to remove. Then click the Remove button in the Question Options box in the lower part of the screen.

Entering Your Own Questions

Test Generator allows you to enter questions you have written to a McDougal Littell Question Bank by adding them to a test folder (see below) or by making your own folder. You can also add or alter questions by copying and editing questions in the Question Bank.

ADDING QUESTIONS TO THE QUESTION BANK

The Edit menu allows you to add your own questions to an existing Question Bank. These options are available when you have the folder for a test highlighted or opened.

The six add options in the Edit menu allow you to create each question type: Essay, Fill-In, Matching, Multiple Choice, True/False, and

```
Add Essay Question
Add Fill-In Question
Add Matching Question
Add Multiple Choice Question
Add True/False Question
Add Modified Matching Question
Copy Question
Edit Question
Delete Question
Add Section
Rename Section
Delete Section
```

Modified Matching. (If these options are grayed or dimmed, you do not have a folder open or highlighted.)

To create an **Essay Question,** click Add Essay Question in the Edit menu. An Edit Question box will open up. Click on the text, "New Essay Question" and then click Edit (a shortcut is to simply double-click on the text). You are now in the Edit Text box. Highlight the text "New Essay Question" and press delete. You can now enter the text for your new question. After entering the text, click on Save. You can now use the same process to enter an answer. Click on the existing Answer text and enter your new answer in the Edit Question box. Click Close when you are finished.

Creating a new **Fill-in Question** is similar to the Essay Question. Click on Add Fill-in Question in the Edit menu. Click on both the Question text and the Answer text and use the Edit Text box to make your changes. Click Close when you are finished.

To create a new **Matching Question,** click on Add Matching Question in the Edit menu. First, add the text of your question by highlighting the words "New Matching Question". Next, click on Answer Options, then Add Left Column Item to add each of the items you would like in the left-hand column. Click Add Right Column Item from the same list to add the items you would like in the right-hand column. To enter your answers, highlight each distractor, click on Answer Options, and choose the correct answer from the list. Click Close when you are finished.

To add a **Multiple Choice Question,** select Add Multiple Choice Question in the Edit menu. In the Edit Question box, highlight "New Multiple Choice Question", click Edit, and add your new text. Next, click on Answer Options and then Add Distractor. When the Edit Text box opens, erase the words "New Distractor" and enter your text. Do this for each of the answer choices. When you have added your distractors, highlight the correct answer and click on Answer Options, then Make Correct. When you have finished, click Close.

To add a **True/False Question,** go to Add True/False Question in the Edit menu. When the Edit Question box opens, click on "New True/False Question", then Edit, and make your changes in the Edit Text box. If the answer to your question is True, you do not need to make anymore changes. If the answer to your question is False, highlight the answer, click on Answer Options, and select Make False. Click Close when you are finished with your changes.

In **Modified Matching Questions** the distractors reside as part of the instruction and sets of modified matching questions all use the same list of distractors. In order to edit the instructions, add distractors, or identify the correct answer for each question, you must first add your questions to a test in the **Your Test** tab. Once your test is built, highlight the instructions in the Your Test tab and click the Edit button. To add a distractor choose Add Distractor from the Modified Matching Options menu and make your changes in the Edit Text box. To identify the correct answer for each question, double click the question in the **Your Test** tab and click on the correct distractor below the heading Other Modified Matching Distractors, then select Make Correct from the Answer Options menu. Click Close when you are finished making your changes. If you are adding several modified matching questions of your own, use the copy question feature. Write your first question and then choose **Copy Question** from the tool bar. This duplicates the instructions and distractors so you'll only need to change the question and answer text. Do this for each question you wish to write.

You can add an exhibit, instructions, or keywords to any type of question by using the Add to Question menu. You can also add an exhibit to answers by using the Answer Options menu. If you choose to add an Exhibit, you will be prompted to choose from the GIF and JPEG files provided with the Question Bank in the Exhibits folder. You may also add your own exhibit if it is saved as a GIF or JPEG file and is placed in the Exhibits folder. When you have finished writing a question, click Close.

Your question will be added at the end of the current folder of the Question Bank. An apple icon designates the question as one you created. To add the question to your test, highlight it and click on Add Question to Test in either the Test menu or the tool bar. To make sure that all of your information is entered correctly, highlight the question and click on the Question Summary tab. You can return to Edit mode if you need to make changes.

A shortcut to editing a question that is already in the Question Bank or your test is to simply double click on the question. This will open the edit box for you.

COPY QUESTION

If you would like to use the text in one question to make a new question, highlight the question and select **Copy Question** from the Edit menu. An Edit Question box will display to prompt you to make changes to the question. When you are finished with your changes, choose Close to add your question to the Question Bank. The Copy Question command will place the copy below the original question and identify the copy with an apple icon.

If you choose Edit Question when an original Question Bank question is highlighted, Test Generator will warn you that you cannot edit an original question. You can then choose to copy and edit the selected question. You cannot, however, change the type a question has been designated as (i.e. fill-in). The new question will be saved in the same test folder and identified with an apple icon.

Note: Original Question Bank questions may have state or national standards associated with them. When you copy correlated questions, the standards are moved from the standards tab into the keywords tab. This is to safeguard against content changes. Once the content of a question changes, the standards may no longer be valid. By leaving them in the keyword field, you may still conduct a search with that information.

EDITING QUESTIONS

Choose which question you want to edit, highlight it, and choose **Edit Question** in the Edit menu or on the tool bar. An Edit Question screen will allow you to change or add to the question. The Edit Question screen displays the text of the question, the instructions for the student, the answer(s) to the question, and the keywords associated with the question. When you copy and edit a question, the keywords tab will list the standards associated with the question.

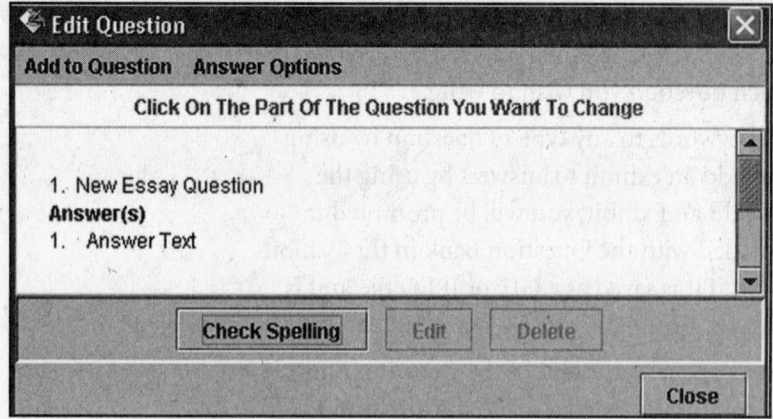

Click on the part of the question that you would like to change and then click Edit (a shortcut is to simply double-click on the area you want to change). When the Edit Text box displays, enter your changes. The symbols at the top of the box allow you to enter your text as plain text, bold text, in italics, or underlined. Just highlight the area of the text you want to change, then click on the corresponding symbol.

You can also insert Special Characters into your text while you are in Edit mode. Click the box on the far left and choose the Special Characters you would like to insert. When you click on the Special Characters, Test Generator pastes it into your text. Click Save after making your changes.

You may want to make additions or changes to your questions while in Edit mode. When you click on the Add to Question or Answer Options menu at the top of the Edit Question screen, Test Generator will give you a list of possible additions and other options. For example, you may want to add instruction, distractors for a multiple choice question, keywords, or an exhibit. If you choose to add an exhibit, the Test Generator exhibit folder will open up. Exhibits are saved as GIF or JPEG files. Choose the one you want and click on open. The File will display in the Edit Question box behind the words Exhibit Path.

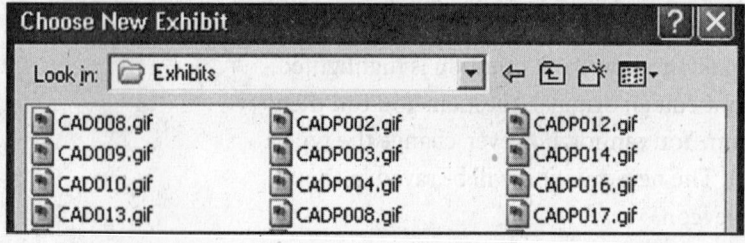

When you have finished making your changes, click Close on the Edit Question box. Your question will display at the bottom of the Question Bank next to an apple icon. Click **Add Question to Test** on the tool bar or from the Test menu to add the question to your test. To make sure that all of your changes are registered, highlight the question and click on the Question Summary tab. The summary will show the text of your question, instructions, answer(s), keywords, and the exhibit.

EDITING INSTRUCTIONS

You can also edit the instructions, point value, and exhibits associated with a question or group of questions. After adding a question to your test, double-click on the instruction text in the Your Test tab. This will open the Edit Instruction screen. Select the text or exhibit you would like to change, then click Edit at the bottom of the screen. You can also delete items by clicking Delete. You may add points or exhibits by selecting from the Add to Instruction menu at the top of the

Edit Instruction screen. Distractors and exhibits for modified matching questions can be added by selecting from the Modified Matching Options menu.

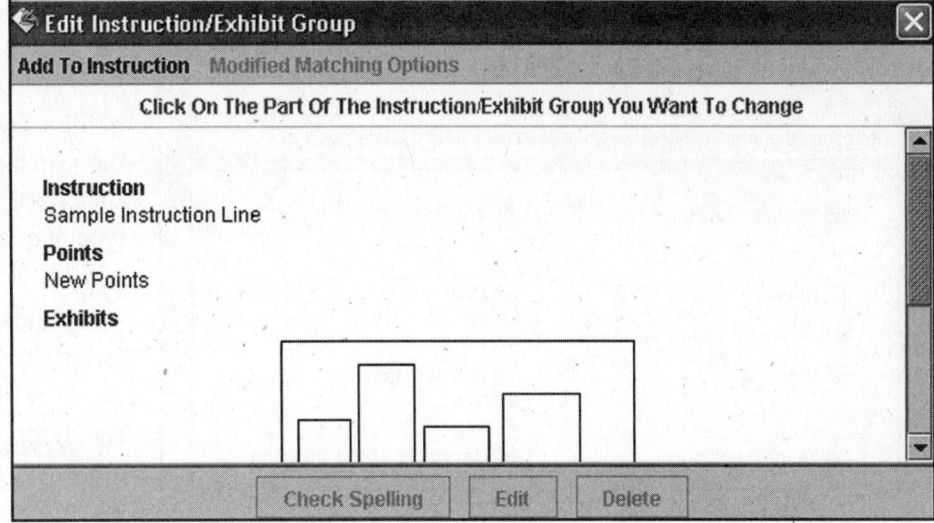

DELETING QUESTIONS

To delete a question from your test, highlight the question and click on **Remove** in Question Options. If you highlight a question in the Question Bank and click **Delete Question** from the Edit Menu, the question will be permanently deleted from the Entire Bank. Test Generator will warn you before making this change.

SAVING CHANGES

After you have entered your own questions and edited them, select **Save Question Bank** in the File menu to permanently save the changes you have made to the Question Bank. If you exit Test Generator without doing this, Test Generator will ask you if you want to save the changes to the Question Bank.

SORT IN BOOK ORDER

Once you have added individual questions to the Your Test tab, you may need to organize the questions in the order they display in the Question Bank. Select **Sort in Book Order** from the Test menu to rearrange the questions. You may also reorder the questions in any manner you choose by simply highlighting them and using the up and down arrows in the Question Options box to move them within your test.

FIND QUESTIONS USING SEARCH QUESTION BANK

The Search Question Bank option helps you browse or search either the entire Question Bank or the Current Section of the bank. You may search for questions of a particular type, that contain specific text, or are related to certain standards.

You can search for questions by type (Essay, Fill-In, Matching, Multiple Choice, True/False, or Modified Matching) by checking or unchecking the appropriate boxes. Any combination of boxes can be checked. Below the text you will see the number of questions included in the search and the number

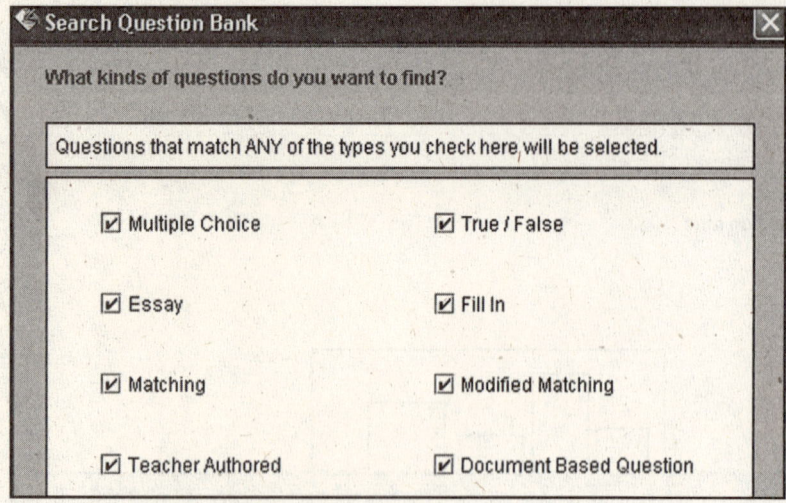

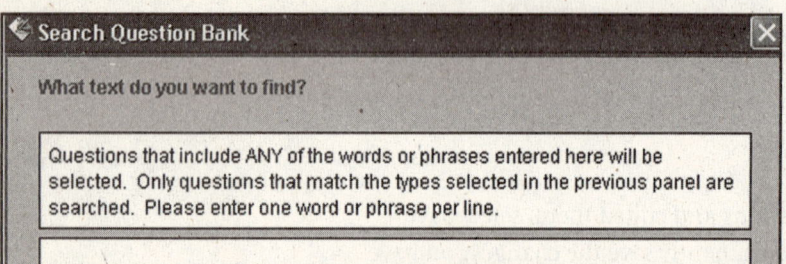

of questions that meet your criteria. This includes all questions that meet any of your criteria. These numbers will change throughout the search process each time you click Apply. After choosing the type of questions you would like to find, click on Next.

The next box will help you search for questions with particular words or phrases. If you want to search for several different words or phrases at the same time, enter one word or phrase per line. Click Next to move on.

Test Generator will next ask for the standard sets you would like to include in your search. All the standards for the Question Banks you have installed will be displayed. Click on the set(s) you would like to include.

Finally, Test Generator will ask which specific standards you would like to find. Again, click on the standards you want to include. When you click on Apply, the number of questions that match your criteria will display in parentheses beneath the list of standards.

When you have finished your selections, click Done.

Your search results will be listed in the Search Results tab on the right. You can highlight a question and click on the Question Summary tab to see each of its parts. Highlight the question in either the Search Results tab or the Question Bank and click Add to Test to include it in your own test.

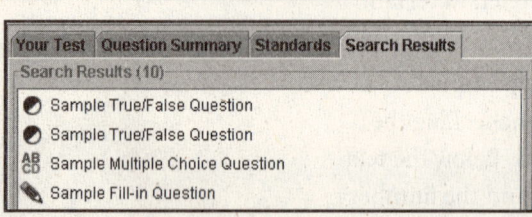

VIEWING STANDARDS

The state or national curriculum standards that may be correlated to the Question Bank(s) installed in Test Generator are listed at the end of the Question Bank

20 TEST GENERATOR USER'S GUIDE

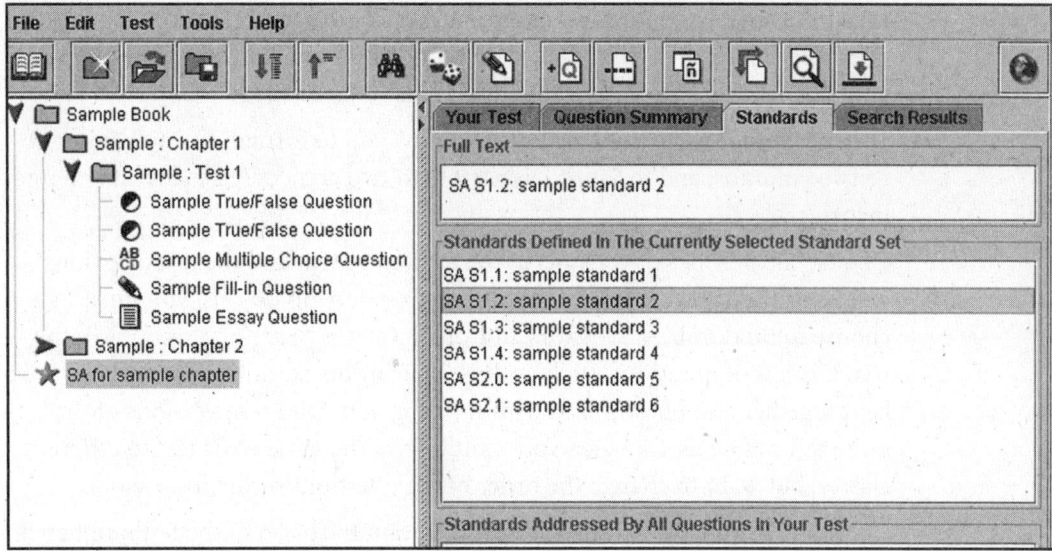

and are designated with the star icon. Click on a star to see the complete list of standards in the Standards tab on the right side of the screen. To read the full text of a particular standard, click on the standard in this scrolling list. If you have a test open, the standards addressed in that test will display beneath the list of standards in the set.

The standards associated with a particular question can be seen by clicking the question in the Question Bank and going to either the Question Summary tab or the Standards tab. You can also click on a question in your own test to see which standards are associated with it. **Remember that if you edit a question the standards will henceforth be listed under Keywords.**

FORMATTING YOUR TEST

Format, accessed from the File Menu, the tool bar, or Test Options, gives you the option to customizing the way a test is formatted. When you select Print Test, Test Generator will give you a last chance to change formatting. After making your changes, click OK.

The **Options** tab gives you several special printing options.

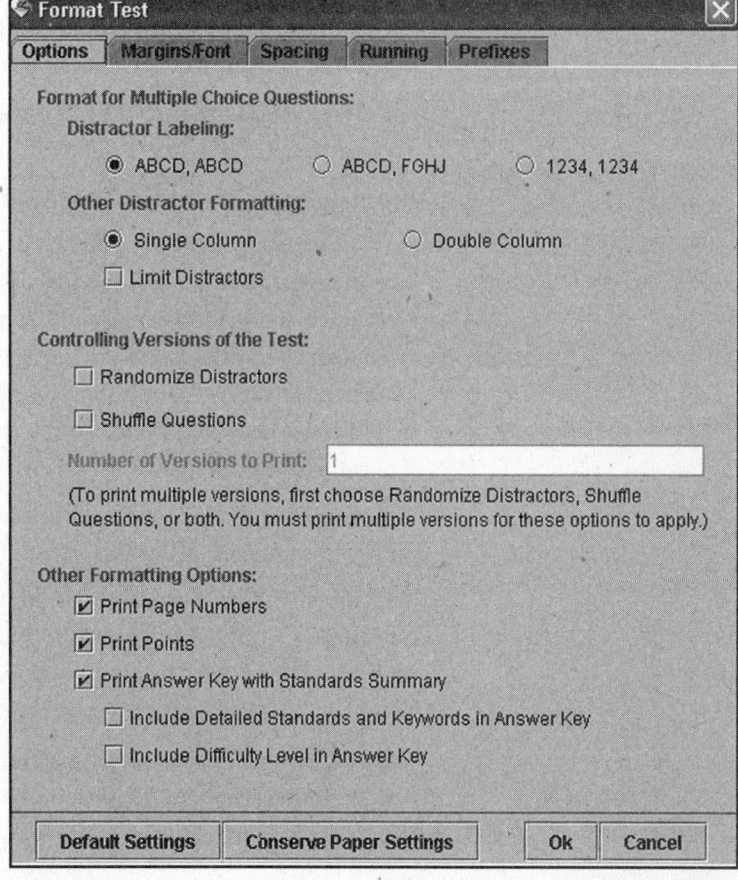

TEST GENERATOR USER'S GUIDE   21

Select the format for multiple choice questions, either ABCD, ABCD (all questions have the choices A, B, C, and D), ABCD, FGHJ (questions alternate with the choices A, B, C, and D or F, G, H, and J), or 1234.

Other Distractor Formatting options allow you to format distractors in one or two columns, and to Limit Distractors to two choices (one correct and one incorrect).

Choose the number of versions of the test, up to ten, and the test questions will be printed in a different order in each version. To do this, you must first choose to randomize distractors and/or shuffle the order of questions in the test. Groups of questions, such as those sharing an exhibit or instruction, are kept together and randomized within that group. Different versions of the same test can be useful when you want to give the same basic test to different classes, but want to change the order of the questions or the distractors.

Check the **Print Page Numbers** box if you want the pages of the test numbered.

Check **Print Points** to print point values included in the question bank. Uncheck this box to hide point values on screen and in print.

Checking the **Print Answer Key with Standards Summary** box will print the answer key and a summary of all the standards met by your test.

Checking the **Include Detailed Standards and Keywords in Answer Key** box will print the answer key, a detailed report of the standards met by each individual question, keywords for each question, and a summary of all the standards met by your test.

Check **Include Difficulty Level in Answer Key** to print the difficulty level of each question. Difficulty level text can be added in the Edit Question screen.

If you do not wish to print an answer key or the standards, uncheck both boxes.

The **Margin/Font** tab sets the margins for your test. The default for Test Generator is one inch on all sides. The minimum margin for most printers is .25 inches. You can also make settings for the header and footer height. The header height must be less than or equal to the top margin, and the footer height must be less than or equal to the bottom margin. The font and the font size can also be changed.

The **Conserve Paper Settings** option automatically adjusts spacing and margins to the smallest allowable size to fit more questions on a page.

The **Spacing** tab allows you to set blank space before and after test items. Essay questions have an additional inch and fill-in questions have an additional half-inch added after the question to allow extra space for the student to answer. You may change the spacing as required for your test.

The **Running** tab shows you the defaults for a printed test. You can change the header, footer, header and footer alignment, and instructions for the first page.

The **Prefixes** tab shows elements that print in a separate column to the left of

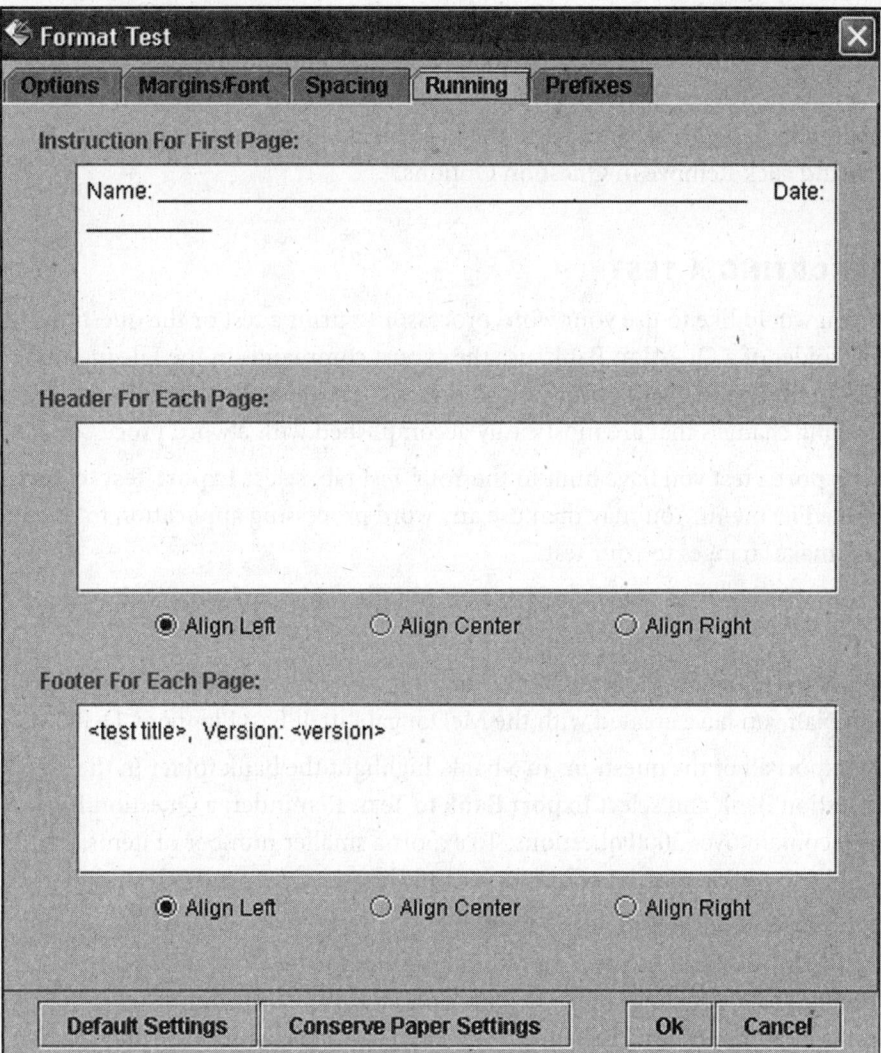

the question number, such as a blank for students to write their answers. Different prefixes for different question types can be entered.

PREVIEW TEST

Preview Test, accessed from either the File menu or the tool bar, allows you to see how your formatted test will appear as a printout. You can choose Fit to Screen to see the entire test page at once, or Actual Size to see the test as it will appear when printed. Click on Next and Prev to move through the pages of your test. It is strongly recommended that you preview your test before printing.

INSERT PAGE BREAK INTO TEST

Test Generator formats tests to make them clear and easy for students to follow. The program determines where page breaks should occur, but some combinations of fonts or font sizes could cause questions to break across pages. If you see this when you preview a test, you can return to the Your Test tab and insert page breaks where needed.

TEST GENERATOR USER'S GUIDE **23**

Click on the test item in the Your Test tab which will be the last question on the page. Choose **Insert Page Break** into Test from the tool bar or the Test menu. You will see the words [*manual page break*] after the question you highlighted. If you need to delete the page break, highlight it in the Your Test tab and click Remove in Question Options.

EXPORTING A TEST

If you would like to use your word processor to print a test or the questions in any folder of a Question Bank, use the export commands in the File menu. You may want to export your test, so that you can make further edits and formatting changes that are most easily accomplished with a word processor.

To export a test you have built in the Your Test tab, select **Export Test to Text** in the File menu. You may then use any word processing application to open and make changes to your test.

Export Test to PDF saves your test as a .pdf file. This can be opened with Adobe Acrobat Reader.

Export Test to EasyPlanner allows you to incorporate a saved test into a lesson plan you have created with the McDougal Littell EasyPlanner CD-ROM.

To export all of the questions in a bank, highlight the bank folder in the Question Bank and select **Export Bank to Text.** Reminder: a Question Bank may contain over 3000 questions. To export a smaller number of items, first build a test with a subset of questions and choose to export the Test, rather than exporting an entire Question Bank.

Publish Your Test Online is a premium service for McDougal Littell customers. It allows you to publish your test to the Web and administer testing options. Students are directed to a web address to take your test which is then scored and reported back to you. For more information see the help menu of your Test Generator program.

Each of these commands write all the questions in the test or folder to a document that is in the Exports folder in the Test Generator folder on your hard drive. Enter the name of the file and click Save. If graphic exhibits are used with the questions, the complete file name of the exhibits will be included in the documents. You can find all graphic exhibits in the Exhibit folder of the Test Generator program.

Changing a Question Bank

CREATING A NEW TEST FOLDER

If you do not want to add your questions to an existing folder within the Question Bank, you can create your own folder. The Add Section command in the Edit menu is available when you have a test folder highlighted or selected. Once you select Add Section, type the name of the new section or folder (such as "Ms. Smith's Questions"), and click OK.

Until questions have been added to the new section, it will have a document icon. To add questions to your test folder, highlight the new section and choose the type of question you want to add from the Edit menu. Use the Edit Question boxes to add the question, its answer, the instruction, and any exhibit or keywords you need for the test item.

After you have added and edited the questions in your section, the section box will change to a folder icon and each of your questions will have an apple icon. If you need to change the name of this section, highlight the section and choose Rename Section from the Edit menu.

If you no longer need a section you added nor all the questions in it, first delete the questions by highlighting each and clicking on Delete Question in the Edit menu. You can then use Delete Section in the Edit menu to remove a test section you have added. If you try to delete a section that has questions, Test Generator will warn you and not allow you to proceed.

IMPORTING TESTS

If you previously wrote test questions in a word processing program, you can use the **Import** feature from the **File** menu of the Test Generator to add those questions to a Question Bank of the Test Generator. In order to use the import command, you must insert special tags of information to your questions using your word processor. These tags are similar to those you would use to create an HTML document. For example, you would insert the tag <qmc> before the text of a multiple choice question.

First, you must save your word processing document with a new name (mytestimport). Next, you'll insert several tags into the document for the questions you have written. This will help the Test Generator to set up the test correctly. Once the file is tagged correctly, save it again as a "text only" file with .imb as the extension (mytestimport.imb).

A special electronic manual is available for those users who want to tag and import their own questions into the Test Generator. For information on the tags and how to set up your import files, please refer to the .pdf file named **Importing_Instructions.pdf** included on your Test Generator CD. Remember, you'll need Adobe Acrobat Reader installed on your computer in order to access these detailed importing instructions.

EDITING QUESTION BANKS

McDougal Littell Test Generator provides a complete Question Bank that accompanies your textbook. You can make changes to the Question Bank by copying questions and editing them. Test Generator safeguards against changes to the original questions and how they may be correlated to state or national standards. The intent of a question may change after being edited and the corresponding standards may no longer apply. Therefore, after you edit a question, the standards related to it are identified as keywords. Editing the Question Bank is one way for you to provide custom questions for students; you can also enter questions that you have written.

Saving Tests

Information for the test you have created is saved in a file for future work. There are four ways to save a test.

Click the **Save Test** button in Test Options on the Your Test tab.

Click the **Save Test** button in the tool bar.

Select **Save Test** from the File Menu.

Use the keyboard shortcut CTRL+S for Windows or ⌘ + S for Macs.

Test Generator will ask you to enter a file name. Enter the name and press Save. Your test will be saved as a .TGT file.

You can select **Save Test As** from the File Menu if you would like to save a test under a new name or in a different location.

OPENING SAVED TESTS

The test documents saved in the Tests folder cannot be opened directly from your desktop. Saved tests can be opened only by starting Test Generator and choosing **Open Test** from the File menu or the tool bar. After opening a test, you may continue to make changes to it or print it. Remember to save the test again if you make any changes to it.

Printing Tests

McDougal Littell Test Generator offers simple options for you to create printed tests. Test Generator gives your tests a professional look. There are many choices available to print a test to your exact specifications, but if you only need a quick printout consult the section on Printing a Test in the Quick Start Guide at the beginning of this manual.

If you would like to print a test from your word processor, rather than directly from Test Generator, use the **Export to Text** feature of Test Generator.

Before printing a test, you must create and save one.

Note: If you are using Mac OS9 or earlier, the test will first open in Adobe Acrobat Reader. In Reader, select Print from the File menu, or click on the printer icon to print your test. If you do not have Adobe Acrobat Reader installed, you may download it for free at http://www.adobe.com.

PREVIEW TEST

Use **Preview Test** from the File menu or the tool bar to view your test as it will appear when formatted. If you click on Fit to Size, Test Generator will shrink your test so that you can see an entire page at once. Actual Size displays the test as it will appear after printing. Click on Prev and Next to move between pages of the test. Click close when you are finished viewing the test.

After previewing your test, click **Print Test** from either the File menu or the tool bar. The Print Test screen will list the specifications of your test and allow you to Change Formatting before continuing. When you are satisfied with the formatting, click on OK.

Help and Technical Assistance

USING HELP

Help is always available from the **Help** Menu of Test Generator. Open the Help Menu to see the list of Help options included in the program.

Click on **User's Guide** to see a PDF file of this User's Guide. You will need to install Adobe Acrobat Reader to be able to read this guide.

Tutorials will walk you through an Overview of Test Generator, as well as the steps to Opening a Test Bank, Formatting a Test, Adding Your Own Test Item, Editing an Existing Test Item, and Searching for a Test Item.

The **Icon Legend** identifies the icon for each question type. You can leave this legend open while you work. Simply use your mouse to move the legend to a convenient place on the screen.

For help with the McDougal Littell Test Generator call 1-800-727-3009 between 9:00 am and 8:00 pm EST Monday through Thursday, and between 9:00 am and 5:00 pm EST on Friday, or visit www.mcdougallittell.com and click on State Resources for updated state standard correlations, troubleshooting information, and patches. For more information about McDougal Littell products, call 1-800-462-6595, or visit mcdougallittell.com.

For help with McDougal Littell Test Generator, call 1-800-727-3009 between 9:00 AM and 8:00 PM EST, Monday through Thursday, and between 9:00 AM and 5:00 PM EST on Friday, or visit www.mcdougallittell.com.

For more information about McDougal Littell products, call 1-800-462-6595, or visit www.mcdougallittell.com.

McDougal Littell

ISBN-13: 978-0-618-37372-7
ISBN-10: 0-618-37372-1

2-72277